Astronauts

By Carmen Bredeson

Consultants
Minna Gretchen Palaquibay
Rose Center for Earth and Space
American Museum of Natural History
New York, New York

Nanci Vargus, Ed.D.
Primary Multiage Teacher
Decatur Township Schools
Indianapolis, Indiana

Katy Kane
Educational Consultant

TOWNSHIP OF UNION
FREE PUBLIC LIBRARY

Children's Press®
A Division of Scholastic Inc.
New York   Toronto   London   Auckland   Sydney
Mexico City   New Delhi   Hong Kong
Danbury, Connecticut

Designer: Herman Adler Design
Photo Researcher: Caroline Anderson
The photo on the cover shows astronaut Michael Lopez-Alegria working
on the International Space Station.

Library of Congress Cataloging-in-Publication Data

Bredeson, Carmen.
  Astronauts / by Carmen Bredeson.
      p. cm. — (Rookie read-about science)
Summary: Introduces the work of astronauts, including special jobs they
might have on the space shuttle and experiments they might perform in
space. Includes index.
  ISBN 0-516-22529-4 (lib. bdg.) 0-516-26956-9 (pbk)
  1. Astronautics—Juvenile literature. 2. Astronauts—Juvenile
literature. [1. Astronautics. 2. Astronauts. 3. Occupations.] I. Title.
II. Series.
  TL793 .B7293 2003   JE
  629.45'0092'2—dc21   BRE
                              C. I   2002011195

$14.25

©2003 Children's Press
A Division of Scholastic Inc.
All rights reserved. Published simultaneously in Canada.
Printed in the United States of America.

1 2 3 4 5 6 7 8 9 10 R 12 11 10 09 08 07 06 05 04 03

Astronauts (AS-truh-nawts)
are men and women who
travel into space.

The first astronauts flew
in small space capsules
(KAP-suhlz). Capsules
are little spaceships.

These little spaceships
held just one person.

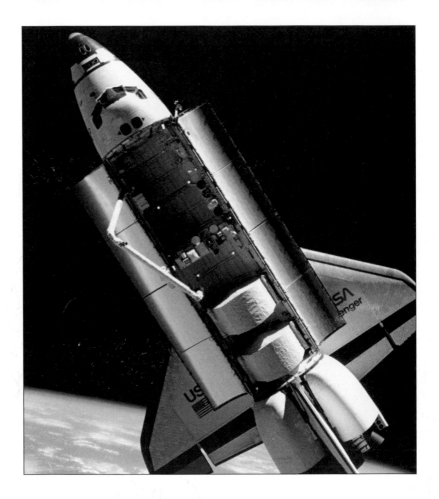

Today, astronauts fly
on the space shuttle.

Eight people can fit inside the shuttle.

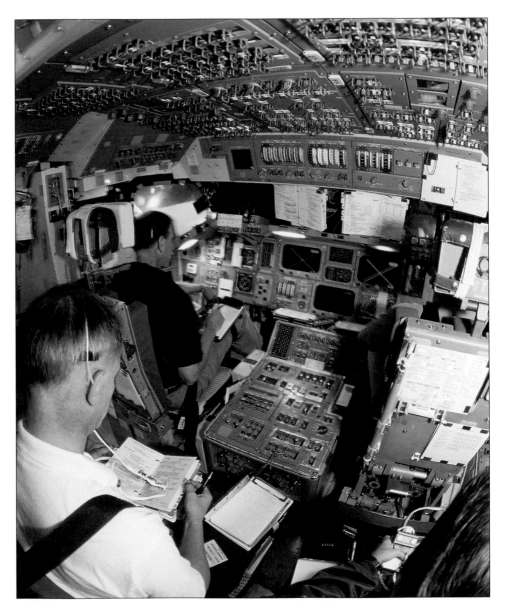

Astronauts train for more than a year to get ready for a flight. They have special jobs to learn.

The commander (kuh-MAND-ur) is the flight leader. This astronaut flies the shuttle. The commander also makes sure the crew is safe.

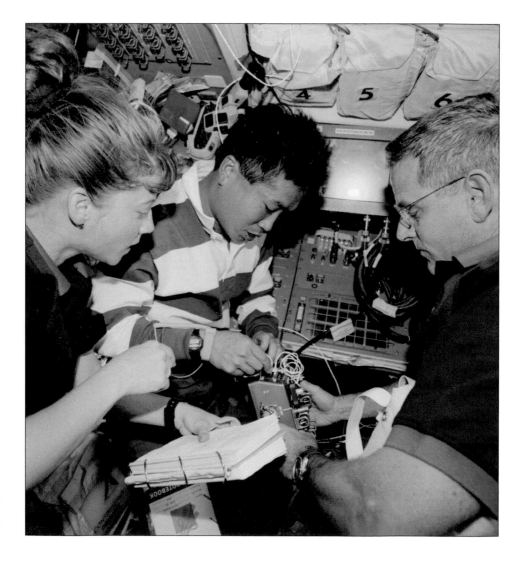

The crew spends months learning how the shuttle works.

What if something breaks in space? The astronauts need to know how to fix it.

Astronauts do science during the flight. Some study how plants grow in space.

15

Sometimes, one of the astronauts is a doctor. The doctor does tests on the crew. The doctor wants to learn what being in space does to their bodies.

Astronauts take space
walks outside of the
shuttle. They put on
big space suits to work
in space.

19

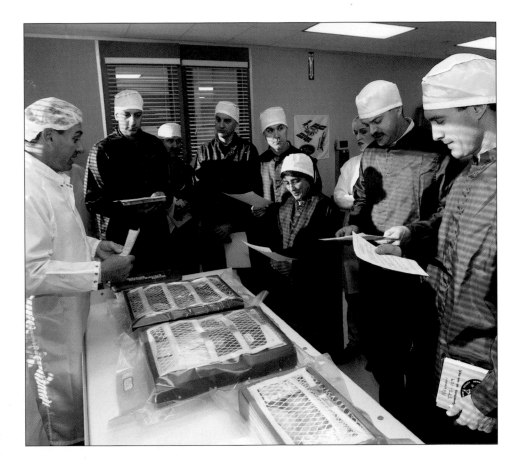

Many astronauts are scientists or doctors. They must have college degrees.

They need to be very
healthy, too.

Do you want to be an astronaut? Study hard in school.

Exercise and eat good food
to make your body strong.

Today there is something new in space. It is the International (in-tur-NASH-uh-nuhl) Space Station.

The whole station will
take many years to build.

A lot of astronauts will be
needed for this work.

Maybe you will be an astronaut.

Will you work on the space station?

Will you be the first person to walk on Mars?

29

Words You Know

astronaut

commander

International Space Station

space capsule

space shuttle

space suit

Index

About the Author

Carmen Bredeson has written dozens of nonfiction books for children. She lives in Texas and enjoys traveling and doing research for her books.

Photo Credits

Photographs © 2003: AP/Wide World Photos/NASA: 5; Corbis Images: 11, 30 top right (AFP), 4, 31 top left (Dean Conger), 29 (Richard T. Nowitz), 7, 8 (Roger Ressmeyer), 3, 6, 16, 22, 30 top left, 31 top right; NASA: cover, 12, 15, 19, 20, 21, 25, 26, 27, 30 bottom, 31 bottom; PhotoEdit/David Young-Wolff: 23.